To Veronica Kelly
Love & peace ⌐
with gratitude

Emey R Tang

鄧
知
平
神
父

1995

Listen, the Clams are Talking

Tenth Anniversary Edition
Revised and Enlarged

by **Hugh Noonan**, Franciscan

Photos by **Emery Tang**, Franciscan

Designed by Ben Lizardi

Library of Congress Cataloging in Publication Data
Noonan, Hugh.
Listen, the clams are talking

1. Meditations. I. Title.
(BX2182.2.N66) 83-732-43
ISBN 0-9612910-0-1

Listen, The Clams Are Talking
(Tenth Anniversary Revised and Enlarged Edition)
by Hugh Noonan, O.F.M., photos by Emery Tang, O.F.M.
Copyright © 1983 Cherry Valley Press

Copyright © 1987 Franciscan Communications
1229 S. Santee St., Los Angeles, CA 90015
Printed in R.O.C.

First Printing   1983
Second Printing 1987

Contents

Acknowledgements

Grateful acknowledgement is given to Franciscan Herald Press, Chicago, for permission to reprint this Tenth Anniversary Edition of *Listen, the Clams are Talking*, and also to include portions from the posthumous publication of his works in *Companion to the Clams*, 1977. The following is taken from that book:

CLAM MYSTERY

Crying
*   while I'm eating clams...*
the clams
*   who gave me the inspiration*
*   for a book.*

I did have a pang.
We had stopped at The Breakers
*   in Morro Bay*
*   and I ordered fried clams.*
I ate them;
*   they tasted very good.*

There is a mystery—how you can reconcile
*   the love of St. Francis for creatures*
*   with the necessity of living.*

The Indians
*   used to apologize*
*   when they killed a buffalo or other animal*
*   for food.*

The creatures
*   are for man's use*
And when they're used rightly,
*   well, it's good.*

Foreword

I never thought I would write a book, especially not this one. When friends started to suggest that these sketches, which appeared originally in our Franciscan Bulletin, should be published, I thought there was not enough body to them—they might make up into something like a Peanuts book—without pictures. Pictures—say, that was an idea! Then somehow it came up that photos would be a natural partner for these musings. This would have to be great photography.

It so happened that I knew just the right man for this creative task. So I knocked on the wall of my room—the Lord arranges these things, for, believe it or not, this photographer, Fr. Tang, has the room next to mine in our friars' house. We talked it over, and he was enthusiastic. We decided that the pictures should not be mere illustrations of the text, but that they should have a life and a dimension of their own.

So that is how the CLAMS got launched.

It's been good working together on this, with one another's contribution as a challenge. The essay would say something about life; the photograph would not repeat the theme, but go on to another dimension. The captions would add another value. So the effect is a three-level commentary identifying with many aspects of life.

I want to thank all those who were tugboats in this operation, especially Miss Juanita Vaughan, who acted as secretary on the project and gave endless hours and her own enthusiasm in making up the manuscript.

Juanita Vaughan and Fr. Hugh Noonan stand outside St. Francis Center, Los Angeles, on opening day in 1972. Still operating and sustained in part by earnings from "Listen, the Clams are Talking," the center has provided food, shelter and clothing for thousands of dependent persons since its founding—yet another legacy of this book's author.

Life, I had a hold on you
            a little while,
        and thought that "mine" was mine to say.
It's such a little while
            since I was young and running,
        and now my life has all but run away.
It's funny how the sun
            grows soft and dear,
        and every leaf you finger with your mind.
I wonder why the past
            comes touched with gold,
        that once was present and I was blind.

Hugh Noonan, O.F.M.
1907-1974
In Memoriam

Her note was blunt, without soul: "Father Noonan died this morning."

The housekeeper had shoved the tiny slip of paper under my guest room door in San Francisco where I was directing a spiritual retreat at a parish.

I remember the stab of resentment I felt against reality and against Hugh. I almost blamed him for dying. He and I had been compiling a second volume, this one on pain, suffering and death. He was going to call it The Hospital Book, a sort of comforting book of musings and prayers for the sick and the bed-ridden. A long-time sufferer himself, Hugh would share with others his discoveries about the precious meaning and value of pain.

But time ran out. And he seemed to know, for the many allusions to the encroachments of sickness, age and death recur through his writings like a steady throbbing.

Ten years later, the book might be entitled, "Listen, Hugh Noonan is Talking." His childlikeness endures and endears. His reflections are timely and timeless. His insights are not admonitions. Rather, they are a sixth sense that enables us to see more, to listen more attentively and to catch more meanings, so to enjoy life to the fullest.

—EMERY TANG

"I'm Glad I Was Here"

A short time before his untimely death of a burst aneurism, Hugh had been interviewed about his thoughts on life and death. During his funeral service, Aug. 6, 1974, his many friends of every rank and file listened to the recording of his remarks.

Q. Tell us your outstanding memories.

Hugh: When I was trying to make life go with only two or three cylinders, I wasn't allowing all of life to be part of myself; I was cutting off whole areas of it. I think it was due to conditioning or tradition, like the Fiddler on the roof, playing the old tune.
But then a period in my life came when I had a great decision to make. It was very late in life (I think I'm a little retarded). It was a very dark time when there didn't seem to be any open end to the tunnel. I didn't know how I could carry my old world into any open, free space of God's creation.

But I hung in there and somehow worked it out. I finally got to understand my creatureness, really to accept God and life, not always trying to remake everybody and everything, and blaming God for not having it perfect. Anyway,—I don't want to sound mystical—it was a very great experience, just like I came out of the rapids or over the shoals, right into open water. And the keel is holding. I'm content with my life and I feel quite fortunate and blessed.

Q. How do you look at people now?

Hugh: I didn't really love anyone with a deep sense until I was well along in years, say, about fifty. Until then I had thought of love as an obligation. We had also been conditioned to think it was dangerous to get involved with people too closely. We lived in a little cloister that we carried about with us.

But now I'm beginning to understand. You've got to keep love circulating. You can't take it for yourself in a complete sense where you own it or possess it or have exclusive rights over anyone. You've got to keep it going.

This discovery has made life a lot more meaningful for me. My life has been enriched with conscious meaning. I think I'm happier now than I was when I was young. I can now love and not be ashamed of it. Love is a sort of feeling, a knowledge that you're worth something, that you're real. Yes, love makes you real.

Q. In the coming years, what would you like to do in the rest of your life?

Hugh: Oh, I don't expect to live very much longer. I have the feeling I won't live much longer. But I'll be happy, I think. My memory's failing. I can't remember my hat. My hearing is growing fainter. I like the films with titles on them now. And I do get tired and sometimes feel a little sorry for myself. But I've got lots to do and I'd like to do it. I'd like to let people grow around me. I want to be able to sense their love and have them live a little better for mine. That's what I'd like, to put it ideally.

Q. What's death going to be like?

Hugh: I think it's going to be real good. But I don't put any features on it; I leave it to Him (God).

Q. What "sound" are you?

Hugh: I think I'm a mandolin, because it adds a little sparkle to life—a little hopeful liveness. A cello is good, too, because that liveness dies if it's not based somewhere. And I've had my share of the lower tones.

Q. If you were to write the epitaph for your own tombstone, what would you want to see on it?

Hugh: I really can't feel it, yet. I can't sum it up that well...the good and the bad...the joyful and the sad. (pause) It's hard to sum up. I'd say:...(pause)...I'm glad I was here.

* * * * *

Note: The simple wooden marker of Hugh Noonan's grave in the Franciscan mission crypt in Santa Barbara bears this epitaph:

> I'm Glad I Was Here.

—and so are we.

💝 💝 💝

Unless you become as little children, you will not hear the voices.

Listen, the Clams Are Talking

I wanted to say something on prayer. I wanted to bring it into focus in our lives. I was fishing for words, but they eluded me. Then I thought of my experience with the clam. That goes back a couple of years, when I was working in television. It was in the making of a TeleSPOT involving a clam. I don't have time to go into details about the television part of it, but I had to get a clam, a four-inch, photogenic clam, because he was the hero of the story.

Did you ever try to locate a large, photogenic clam? It's not easy. Well, I thought I might as well start at the top. I called a friend of mine, who happened to be president of a large fish company. His name was Louie, and he was in the middle of an executive conference. I thought he might have peculiar reactions when I asked him over the phone if he could get me a large clam—heh! heh! But he was immediately solicitous. He said he wasn't personally acquainted with any large clams, but he had quite a few connections in the business. I should call Nick, who was big on clams.

So I called Nick. Nick told me he had lots of clams in his freezer, but that they were only two and a half inches. What I would need would be a Quahog clam. They were only available in Chesapeake Bay, but he would have them put one in his next truck-load of Eastern clams. I told him it would have to be more than one—we always need a stand-in for TV and that we couldn't wait that long—we were shooting the next day. He said, "Call Harry at the Central Market. He's up on the clam situation—and, by the way, Father, I've quit going to church. But I don't feel good about it. A priest bawled my wife out for coming to Communion in slacks. We were on vacation, and it got me mad." So we talk about that. I told him that one swallow does not a summer make, nor does one priest a Church make. He seemed relieved.

I called Harry at the Central Market. His clams were too small—and he hadn't been to confession in years. He couldn't get up nerve to go into that dark box. So we talk about that.

Then I call Ben, a gourmet restaurant manager. He tells me he has to take clams off his menu—they are too expensive, and people won't order them—and, by the way, he has a retarded son. The boy had been in a job that kept him happy, but that work had run out, and he couldn't find that type of job and had become seriously disturbed. So we work on that. (Actually it turned out well, and he was very thankful). He told me to call Sam's Restaurant—"They grow clams in the back yard"—and he would be able to help me.

I call Sam's and the hostess answers: "Did you wish reservations?" Embarrassing! But there's no backing out now. "Yes, in a way—I want to reserve a large clam." She doesn't bat an eye on the phone. She says, "Just a minute, Father, I don't know about clams myself, but I'll ask Sam." She comes back and says, "Our clams are too small—and, by the way, do you have a minute, Father?" She is in a predicament. Her boyfriend wants to get married, and he has two years more of college, and she would have to work and she loves him, but what to do? So we go into that.

After that, I got acquainted with Einar. He called me up to say he had a three and a half inch clam. Sam had phoned him. I said, "Einar—I never came across that name before." Einar said, "I'm a Finn." It developed into an ecumenical conversation. He said, "I never talked to a Catholic priest before." I said, "I never talked to a Finn before. What goes on with the Finns?" He came back with: "I never expected to meet a priest in the fish business." I answered, "The first priests were fishermen." Say! He got real friendly after that! And he did have a big clam—three and a half inches.

The phone rang again. It was Nick: "I heard you got your clam. But I've got clams as big as his—and I'm closer."

I was amazed: "How did you know about Einar?" Well, Louie had talked to Nick, and Nick had talked to Sam, and Sam had talked to Einar, and the hostess at Sam's got into it, and they all ended up talking together.

I'm sorry to say the clam itself didn't go anywhere. The TeleSPOT never got off the beach. But it taught me something about my job as a priest. If I had approached all these people on the level of "Where were you last Sunday? You must observe the law. Love thy parish priest. Marriage is a sacred sacrament. Repent and be saved"—if I had done that, I'd still be standing at the church door. Borrowing a clam—that's crazy. But it was human, and it touched life.

Clams were a real part of the life of these people. That is what prayer should be to us. They were clam people; we should be prayer people. Our life should be geared to prayer. We talk about devotions and saying prayers, like hanging pictures on a wall. But prayer has to be *in* the walls. The house of our being must vibrate with it. The presence of Christ should be as real to us as a boy-friend, or a flare-up of anger, or a fear of the unknown. Prayer is not an alien walk in a strange land. It is a turn around the block in our own neighborhood where we are one with other people and with God.

ṽ ṽ ṽ

Behind walls you will often find something weak and frightened waiting to be help

Whose Sunny Afternoon

Exposition Park is one of my favorite places. It's close to St. Joseph's here in Los Angeles, and it's a different world. The other day I had an hour or so off, so I drove over there and parked near the rose garden. By the way, that's a place to see. Acres of roses and all blooming now—a little past bloom, to be truthful—but the place is full of color. It's a lovely spot.

And people *walk* there. Not like in streets and stores and offices, where they are either running or sitting with empty eyes.

Anyway, I joined the walking people, and began to pick up their rhythm. Who were these people who would come on a Sunday afternoon to walk among the roses? Well, there were Indians—from India, I mean—Orientals, black people, many Latins, a few Anglos. There were many family groups, and their appearance said, "low income," "underprivileged."

As I was walking—not minding my own business—I passed a corner of this enclosure, and there was a little boy sitting on a sandpile left over from the gardener's work—a little black boy, of four or five. He was sitting there, and I came along. He said, "Hello," and I said, "Hello." You could see he was a philosopher, from the way he was observing things. The little boy looked at me in a thoughtful way, and he said, "Sir, do you own the park?"

I stopped and looked at him. I didn't know what to say. He was waiting for my answer, and all I could think of to say was, "No, I don't own the park."

I guess I looked as if I came from a different world. I thought I was dressed pretty casually, but that's still better than most of the people in the park.

I've been sorry ever since that I didn't go farther into this conversation. I might have learned something. I wish I had said to the little boy, "No, I don't own the park. The city owns it. But the park doesn't really belong to the city. It belongs to the people."

I'm supposed to be a poor Franciscan. But I don't know what it is to be poor the way these people know it—and that goes for that little boy and his family, wherever they are. You see, my kind of poverty is something I chose for myself. I wasn't trapped into it by greed or injustice, as most of the people in the park have been trapped. I'm content to do without a lot of things. But these people are fighting to escape a poverty that means run-down houses, slave jobs, not enough food or clothes for themselves or their children.

It's easy for me—and for you, my friends, who are better off—to get soft, closed off even in our attempts to be of value in the world. It happens if we don't mix with people and really identify with them. We begin to act as if we own the park.

No, we don't own the park. We don't really own anything we have. Everything is a gift to us from God.

Those people in the park—they had a waiting quality about them, a drifting, a knowing that tomorrow they would go back to a rough world and a hard life. And many of them go unhealed by the balm of hope, the touch of Christ in their lives.

The only way we can thank God for his gifts to us is to share them with our brothers—like the little boy and the others in the park. The greatest things we have to share are God's love and Christ's word. God's sky, his grass, his flowers, birds and trees he gives to everybody. But his love comes only from man to man, as it came from Christ our brother to us. It's the only possession that we can give and still keep. The more love we give, the more we have.

"No, little boy, I don't own this place—or anything else. Nobody does. Nothing is really ours, except the power, the privilege, and the blessing of sharing."

But I didn't say this to the little boy. He wouldn't have understood much of it, anyway. But I'm wondering now—will anybody talk to him this way when he is old enough to understand? I wonder, too—by that time, will he have any patience left to stand and listen? That will depend on what has been given to him—and the people like him in the park—by those of us who call ourselves the followers of Christ.

When we will learn
to love as a flower loves—
by giving freely of its fragrant self—
there will be
Peace on Earth
at last.

No Mermaids Sing to Me

I like a tugboat. It's nothing great to look at, but it takes on impossible tasks. The Princess Italia may proudly ride the imperial seas, but when she gets into tight waters, the tugboat comes churning up to take over. There's one churning up the channel now (I'm on the pier at Terminal Island, and I like that word "churning"). The life of the sea would stop without tugboats. In the sunsets of every port in the land, tugboats are the poetry of coming home, and they point great ships to the open sea. I like the way they stick their snoot up in the air and say, "I'm here to serve and proud of it."

We could learn something from that. Tugboats are the energizers of greater things than themselves. But they don't get much recognition. Who ever heard of a tugboat getting showered with confetti or streamers, or having flower wreaths on its poop deck? Their wreaths are beat-up tires—for bumping purposes only.

The liners come sailing in, grandly, with the smell of far-away places on them, and the glamour. There's nothing stylish about a tugboat. It has a hand-me-down look. With its old gear, it looks like a mechanic who comes in at the end of a day's work with grime in his fingernails and his pores.

Sitting here on the wharf, watching the tugboats, now why should I start thinking about my brother Vin? He was the oldest in our family. He only went to the seventh grade. He had no gift for books; he didn't spell very well, and his handwriting was large and labored, like a child's. But he had a feel for tools—he was a mechanic—and he was something more. He was a poet at heart. When he came home at night, he would teach me to recite simple poems. We all slept, our family of five boys, in one sleeping porch out almost over the Western Pacific tracks in Sacramento. A lot of sleeping went on in that one room. But Vin and I would be huddled with our books, under the light that he had rigged up himself over our double bed. He would still smell of machinery, of the cars that he worked on, and he would still be grimy. But in those nights I developed a great love of poetry. And, through poetry, the beginnings of whatever understanding I have of the beautiful things in life.

One poem that I remember especially was "The Spell of the Yukon." I recited that one night at dad's union meeting. He was secretary of the union. I was seven or eight at the time, and I remember the awe of being allowed into this forbidden land. It was a men-only thing, a "smoker." The men were drinking beer, and they had pitchers of oysters swimming in tomato juice. When they put some in a mug for me, I was horrified. But when

I closed my eyes, the oysters slid down by themselves. The thrill was tremendous. Life was a whole new adventure.

Anyway, those big, rough men—railroad linemen they were—lifted me up on the chairman's table and got me to recite "The Spell of the Yukon." And I can still remember the opening-out of life on that occasion—the roar of approval, the big hands clapping, and my dad so proud. I think that might have given me confidence I would never have had otherwise in life. Out of such things are lives made. And it was my brother Vin who had nudged me into that adventure. Like a tugboat. But I realize now that I never really thanked him for it.

Looking back at my brother Vin, long after his passing, I think he had a lot of St. Francis of Assisi in him. He just wanted to be at peace with everyone, to be a part of life without hurting anyone. He was very courteous, in a clumsy sort of way. He would open doors and do kind things in a shy, apologetic manner, making a joke of his clumsiness. He was very content to work without recognition—well, no, he wasn't. He liked attention; he liked someone to talk to. But few people really noticed him, or thanked him for anything he did.

I could tell you a lot about my brother Vin. Sometimes I envy him. I don't envy him his lack of confidence and his lack of advancement. I found out later on that he felt very inadequate. But I do envy him the greatness that he had and that wasn't appreciated. As I grew older, I realized that he wasn't so gifted. Yet he had so much of what the world needs. I don't know how I got him mixed up with tugboats, but I'm glad I did. He deserves some kind of thanks for those nights on the sleeping porch that pushed me into an understanding of life and an appreciation of beauty. And he's still pushing. I should pray for him more often.

Sometimes people who do the greatest service don't get much recognition. But they're missed when they're not there.

This meditation is dedicated to all unappreciated people. Who are they in your life? Go back along the corridor of your life, and see them standing against the wall—silent, closed, unthanked. These people aren't able to show their disappointment. You could easily forget that they feel the hurt. They spend their lives pushing and doing and helping. Quiet, almost passive, but giving so much.

Let's you and me pray: "Lord, forgive me all my sins of unappreciation, especially toward those who have done so much for me, and have been recognized so little, and have been thanked by me hardly at all." Join with me in this prayer, because I'm sure there are tugboats in your life.

SHIP: *This is embarrassing.*
Couldn't you wait until after dark?

TUGBOAT: *This is no time for temperament.*
The tide is running.

SHIP: *If you just looked a little more respectable...*

TUGBOAT: *Do we have to go through this every time?*

SHIP: *I've made it on my own all the way from Sydney,*
and it's been a rough go.
I deserve a little respect.

TUGBOAT: *Don't fuss. So you're tired.*
We'll make you look good at the dock.

SHIP: *Oh—(blasting mightily) Los Angeles,*
here comes the Pacific King!

TUGBOAT: *Big deal!*

Which goes to show that even the biggest of us
needs some help from our little friends.

See the man with the dog.
The man is blind.
The dog's name is Gertie.
They go every place together.
They walk very fast through the crowd.
They go to the restaurant together.
Everybody knows Gertie.
Gertie lies under the table.
The waiter brings a plate and says,
"The rice is at 9 o'clock, Ray."
He means it's on the left.
I wish I had a dog like Gertie.
I hope they will have a long time together.

But Then There Was Bomba

Father Sylvester was telling me about his experience in the pet cemetery. He was amazed at the way people were drawn together. They were weeping on one another's shoulders. Emotions were strong and visible. Husband and wife were very close, comforting each other. Children were crying together, for once at peace with one another. There were flowers all around, and soft music. And there was one gravestone that said: "Sweetheart, wait for me." (ick!)

He said that he had never seen emotion as strong as that in a human cemetery. That's a funny thing. Do people like pets more than people? Yes, it seems so.

Why is that? Well, people—you and I—like to be loved without question, and we don't want to pay the price of loving in return. A dog adores its master. The master can do no wrong. The master has unlimited power. He says to the dog, "Come," and the dog comes. "Go," and he goes. "Roll over," and he does it. A dog makes no demands. We can't possess people. And often that's too hard for us to take. Sentiment is cheap; love is dear. We expect people to accept us as unquestioningly as a dog does—that's the trouble with our kind of love, isn't it?

But, on the other hand, as Topol says in "The Fiddler on the Roof," there was Bomba. Bomba was a dog I had when I was teaching in the seminary. He was black, and he did have a glossy coat. But that's about all you could say about him definitely. He was under middle size. His pedigree was dubious— no Daisy Hill Puppy Farm in his background—I got him out of the pound. But he was mine.

He followed me everywhere. He slept in my room, followed me to class, and waited at the door. He might even have kept awake during my lectures. Nobody else counted but me. He was friendly to others, but I was Number One. Some in our Community of Franciscan Friars didn't like Bomba, I couldn't figure that out, because he was very gentle.

He was smart, too. He could open doors (what's a few scratches around the door knobs?) and he could drink out of a pop bottle. I was learning to play golf at the time. Bomba was a terrific caddy. I'd hit practice balls on the baseball diamond, and he'd bring them back—all of them. He never lost a ball. One day I tried him on a golf course. He retrieved 35 balls, only some of them really were not lost. There was some bad language when golfers couldn't find their balls that surely had landed on the green. Bomba was very enthusiastic, but I thought we had better leave the scene. He never did get to know which balls were the "lost" ones.

When he got distemper, I watched at his bedside—my bed—like a doting mother. He was so sick, poor little guy, and I nursed him back. His hot nose was clogged with mucus; he couldn't lift his tired head from his paws, but his eyes, filled with puzzlement and pain, followed me all the time.

Bomba never hurt a flea. I think he had a few. Scratching is a sign of either nervousness or fleas, and Bomba wasn't nervous.

But tension came in the Community over Bomba. For instance, they, "the jealous ones", accused him of "doing things" on the stairs. But it was obvious from the size of the "things" that they must have been done by the cat. Bomba was always thoughtful about those matters.

Then I went off to war,—No. II—and Bomba had to go to a foster home. I think it was about a year later that I got back on furlough and went to see him. He seemed integrated, and didn't recognize me at first. But, after a bit, he began to act uncertain. Then suddenly he came over and put his head on my knee, very contented. I thought afterwards how selfish that was of me—to separate him from his new family and make him start over again.

Since then, I never have gotten too close to pets. And when I look back, I see that I made a big mistake in soaking up all Bomba's love. Besides, I allowed him to separate me from people. But I still have a fond memory for Bomba. He was real, and maybe he was a symbol. Next time around, I would still love Bomba, but maybe I could share him.

How did this get to be a Christmas message? I don't know. Except perhaps that it is a meditation on love. Love can separate, love can hurt. But love shared is Christmas.

Bridge Over Troubled Space

Shakespeare said, "I could be bounded in a nutshell and count myself king of infinite space."

"Space" is a funny word. Look at it. SPACE or S P A C E. It can be long or short, depending on how you look at it. And how you treat it.

Space is news nowadays, good news and bad news. It means open, free, like "home on the range, where the buffalo roam" or closed, dead, like the emptiness we have created in parts of Vietnam.

Space can be a box, a box that you hide in because you are afraid of freedom. You box yourself off from other people in an elevator, in a church—a great, big church where space is used to separate people instead of bringing them together.

You can put space around other people, to box them in. "They're all right as long as they stay in their place." But you can also give a person a box of peace which he needs in order to grow. Some people can't stand too much space. They are not ready yet.

Space has good and bad uses, but it is really a gift of God. It is a place where our lives happen.

Space can be freedom, room to stretch. It has lots of potential. It is life-giving, exhilarating. But other people have space also. You have to be careful not to take up their space, not to interfere with their freedom. You can penetrate it to bless it, to help it, to charge it with life, friendship and compassion, but not threaten it, and not to crowd it. Space is where you are, and it has a lot to do with the way you are.

Space has to be used wisely. For example, space can give you quiet; it can give you associations, moments of happiness, love, joy. It can give you beneficial regret, contrition. Space can do these things for you by the opportunity that it extends, by the sounds that are heard in that place, by the airs that blow there.

Space, in a sense, is relationship. Space is nothing unless there are at least two to share it. You drop over the edge into nothingness if you are alone. Space has no meaning without the crisscross web of human relationship. The only time to be alone is when God is there. And that is not alone. You have a guest from outer space.

Space does separate people physically. This is unavoidable. But love is a bridge over troubled space. It will not allow separation between people who love one another.

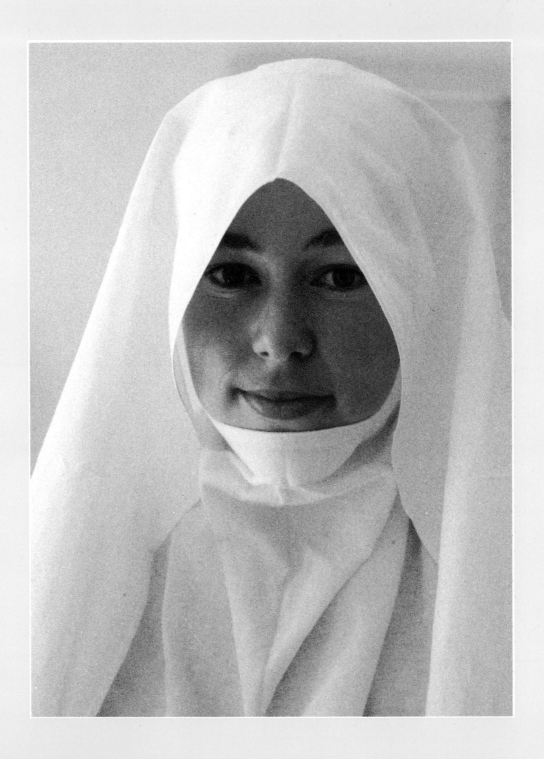

When a person is open, he can go as far as he wants in space. All outdoors, all the universe is his. As far as he can reach, space stretches out above him. But "if a soul is flat, the sky will cave in on him by and by."

Space is mystery. It pushes you out in all directions.

Space is a tremendous gift, but we have to learn how to use it. I must remember this—that space has no meaning unless you put something good in it, like prayer. You need to create a little pocket of prayer, a space in which God has a special home, a space of quiet which expands your spirit.

Life gets crowded with many things. Minds tend to become attics jumbled with all kinds of thoughts. Space is a gift from God. Save some of it for Him.

You are standing
on the same earth
that I stand on.
Our roots touch;
the same rain
runs together between us.
I touch you
through the air;
we share the sun.

You push your space
and you come into mine.
Not what is gone
or to come.
Now. Humming in the ground.
Walk strong.
I feel you
in my standing straight.

You are old and worn, Granny White, like the hills around you.
You look out at life without expectation but without fear.
You have had happy times, but not many.
And you have died all the deaths there are—death of scrounging in the dirt and the cold,
and death of men with the black lung, and death of the land under the strip mining machines.
But you hold on, you endure, without knowing exactly why.
Your God presses down hard, but he is just, and his love must be somewhere.
You still smile once in a while—when you see a baby.

On the Other Hand

Peace...Peace...Peace...If we could only live without tension...

I'm sitting here in Melody Park, one of my favorite meditation places. I came for peace and quiet. So what...a locomotive, half a block away, is pulling its load on the tracks along Washington Boulevard. It's blaring its way along like a sick cow, blowing, blowing, blowing, and I want peace and quiet. Then I think—if they didn't blow that horn, they'd be knocking over cars and killing people. So I've just got to put up with the noise. So I do.

And it occurred to me that peace is not an absence of tension; peace is the handling of it, being able to keep your balance when life pushes you this way and that. Peace of heart is a balance point between opposites—between yes and no, up and down, east and west, between the devil and the deep blue sea, or between God and mammon.

Everyone has tensions. The old: "I can't take care of myself much longer, but I don't want to go to a rest home." The young: "I'm trying to live in two worlds, my parents' and my friends.'"Parents: "Love is knowing when to let go but they need me." The sick: "The doctor says I'll have to learn to live with it." The successful: "Shall I stay where my family is happy or take the promotion?"

That there should be no tension in life,—I guess that's fantasy—out of this world. Who that was real ever lived without it? Surely not Christ, who had the pull between the will of his Father and the stubbornness of men, who had the wanting to rest and the call to the cross.

And the tension in the life of St. Francis of Assisi—a tremendous desire for the life of quiet, of aloneness with God and, on the other hand, the need that men had of him and his need to be with men. What a tension: he never conquered it completely, but he came closer to peace than any of us will ever come. Can you imagine St. Francis without tension? He argued with the law of gravity.

Tension...high tension...high tension wires...the Wichita lineman. My dad was a lineman, and he wrestled with high tension, with danger, most of his life. He was always between the danger and the need to earn a living for us. He got injured on the high line just before he retired, but he managed. And I'm here to remember it.

In the good old days, we used to live and die with Notre Dame. One of the brethren, a good friend of mine, couldn't stand it when USC played Notre Dame. He would come into the radio room, and he'd ask: "What's the score?" We'd fill him in on the game, and he'd jump up and say, "I can't stand it! I can't stand it!" He'd go out and run around the grounds. Five minutes later, he'd stick his head in the door for another report. He just couldn't listen to the play, but he had to know the score. What exquisite torture! Later I think most of us began to realize that the Lord wasn't building his kingdom on football but in the hearts of men, and in deeper ways. So the tension was reduced. But sometimes the old feeling comes back.

Tension is a stretching process. We are stretched on a cross; we are stretched to draw out of us the things God wants, be it acceptance or bravery. If we could only see it in that light, we would have the wisdom and incentive to deal with it.

Tensions are not easy to manage. Let's think this out. I guess we should study our own particular tension first. Take a piece of paper and write down: "This is my tension," etc., etc. It might help. Then measure it, not against today but against the day after tomorrow. I mean, if you take only today, it might be just a passing mood. Don't let too much be expected of you. Impossible dreams, yes; impossible demands, no. Love builds up, obligation wears down. Be honest. Pull the mask from the face of your challenge. In all tensions, pray. Prayer is the between-power. It takes two seemingly opposite realities and makes them one. Life prayed is life lived. In the gigantic loneliness of being human and having problems too big for you, His is the only voice that can say "Peace."

From all of this, you could think that I am an expert on reducing tensions (for headache, take aspirin; for simple tension, take Fr. Hugh). Oh, no, I wish I were. Take today, for example. It's my day off. I'm under doctor's orders to get out for golf (it took me a long time to find that doctor.) But there is a writing deadline to meet—it's waiting for me. I just can't let people down. There is only one way to go. But, on the other hand, this is the day when I really think I'm ready to beat Father Emery at golf...

The Voice of Many Waters

I was walking down the hall in our friary the other day and I heard a sound from the water cooler. Glumph! It was an inadvertant burp. That happens, you know. I looked at the water in the bottle and I felt sorry for it. So I decided it was time we had a little talk. 'Oh, water in the bottle, that sound makes me feel sad. You're clear, but you're sterile. And it's bad to be cooped up like this. You used to be first, but now you're last. Coffee, tea, beer, cola, Uncola—they all come ahead of you. "You used to sound like something. And here you are in a bottle, and people come and push a spigot, and your only sound is "glumph, glumph, ickle, ickle."

I have heard you when you were the sea off San Diego; I stood on the railroad track above the beach. It was a gray evening of rain and clear. A dark cloud brooded south of the sun's leaving. You were the sea and you were silver, coming in, coming in. And I heard your sound. There was a kind of labored breathing in the surf, and your sound was "huh, huh, huh, quash, quash," questioning and quieting the land. O water, you are mystery. You speak a language very deep—below words—something hidden from the ages, hidden from the beginning of the world, like the voice of God, shaking and hushing the lives of men.

We must come from the sea. Our tears are salt.

And I have heard you in the green mountains, shouting down the gorges, leaping, laughing in the rapids—that was jubilee road. I remember you in Lake Aloha, high in the Sierras, with the skeletons of trees standing still in your depths, a hundred feet down, and the song you sang in that high, thin air was like Easter morning.

I have stood at my window, watching you in the rain. How good you sounded on the roof, and how good you felt when you insinuated yourself into my dried-out spirit! What if the day was sullen? The sunlight was being washed and made new again.

If love could be
   as enduring
      as clear, cool water in a pool
Water accepts you totally
Its embrace is complete
It touches every surface of your body
   and of your spirit
Passion is in fire
   and good too
But water is for calm
It sustains you
   if you trust it
But never let water
   get tired of you

Give it back
   your joy
Move to its rhythm
Never become a rock
   or love will let you go
Love is a flow
   a touch
      an embrace

Love is mating beyond bodies
   beyond marriage
      beyond time
Love is like water

Of course, you don't always look so pretty. You don't look so good in the bathtub. You're all dirtied up. But then I realize that you are dirty that I might be clean. You wash not only my feet but my head and my hands. You are very kind to put yourself through that. It's a sign of caring. I beg your pardon, and I thank you. Especially when I think how great and strong you are in the waterfall, and throwing thunder bolts around the sky and the like.

O water, you can also be a flood, a raging anger in the universe. I don't understand that. But everywhere you are cleansing, if we can accept your mystery. And you do end in a rainbow.

Incidentally, you surely make it hard for the weatherman. Do you resent being predicted? Instead of looking embarrassed on TV all the time, he should get on good terms with the water in his body—they say humans are 56 percent water—and he would get closer in his predictions, because he could *feel* the weather. (This is a new theory I'm developing.)

But to return to reality. This is awesome—I am *swimming* in existence. O water, you hold together whatever is me, and I share your security and your tides and your storms. You need redemption like me, but if I could learn to know God in your sacrament and in your pulsing prayer, I would live as I have never lived before.

But now I must come up for air. In our down-to-earth world, you are both good news and bad. But bad only when we use you wrongly. Light water is dew, sparkling on the grass—what a lovely world it makes! Heavy water is the hydrogen bomb. You sustain us and you test us.

I'm sorry I gave you a bad time for being in the bottle. Maybe this is the only way that you can come into our Coke-eyed world to save us.

St. Francis of Assisi, whom I admire very much, once called you "Sister Water—so useful, humble, precious and pure." I wish I could just say that and be glad. That's a prayer.

A Walk on the Golden Water

I am in Exposition Park, in the shadow of the Coliseum, at the edge of the USC campus in Los Angeles. I am parked in one of the little winding streets. I came here to get away from the hullabaloo that crowds the life of all of us these days. I have put a nickel in the meter—yes, there are parking meters here among the trees. Ahead of me a little ways is a blunt stop sign. Over to my left is an old, deserted place that was once a bandstand. It looks almost like the Acropolis—it is something out of the past. And there are garbage cans here and there on the grass.

The low sun is flowing across the grass, very softly, like golden water. An occasional car comes by and pulls the autumn leaves behind it, like dry bones coming to life. As the car moves on, the autumn leaves settle down again.

Life is movement, I guess. There is very little stillness anywhere except deep within the human heart. And it is hard to keep stillness there.

It is quiet here in the center of the city, in the center of the youth generation. It is quiet, finally.

A couple of young people walk across the grass, silhouetted against the sun. Even they are quiet. A question: why do we not work harder at getting a little quiet for ourselves, a little solitude in the midst of living—a stillness in the center of our being?

(Lord, you have given us this world for the sun to flow gently on. And we need parking meters, stop signs, an empty Coliseum, autumn leaves, student couples walking around wrapped in their own thoughts. They walk around the refuse cans. These couples walking, holding hands—let's not imagine all the secret, dark things they might be thinking. In this violent world they live in, holding hands may be one of the things that makes the best sense. Help me to be at all times open to the mystery of your love, and not to let it get squeezed out by all the things that are.)

The sun has just gone behind the trees, but it said, "I'm the sun," before it went down.

Walking across the grass is a great experience. It's two people with space around them. Two people walking on the golden water.

There is a dog now, lost in wonder, looking around like a sailor at sea, launching into a run, just for the pure joy of having room. Running in circles on the grass. But he should have a boy with him, or at least another dog. What's running room without someone to share it? Or maybe the grass will be for him only a place to do his solitary business.

What I am trying to say—and the dog makes it clear—I am trying to say that nobody is anybody without somebody else. The sun throws rays across the grass, and the people catch them in webs of meaning. The whole world means nothing, even with the sun, unless people are joined together by the shining wires that connect their lives.

Garbage cans and stop signs and golden lawns are all mixed up in a meaning. If only two people were in that Coliseum over there, it would have a meaning.

It's evening now. I'm glad I put a nickel in the parking meter and bought thirty minutes of quiet to sit here and see the mystery of God shining out in the crisscross lightings of an ordinary day.

The First Million Years

Vacation was interesting this year. I had a talk with a mountain. This wasn't just any old mountain—this was one of the Canadian Rockies. (I have a postcard here somewhere.) It's not too easy to get together with mountains. They always kind of look down on you. And mountains are not exactly noted for conversation, either.

As a matter of fact, I found these mountains inclined to be grumpy as well as lofty. Our conversation went like this:

Me: "There you are, standing up over me, with your head in the sky. You are very impressive. You look like the patient glory of God. But you're kind of craggy and full of rough spots. For all your glory, you're kind of unfinished."

Mountain: (By the way, mountains speak low and very, very slow. If it weren't for my recorder-mind, and my instant, speeded-up replay, I couldn't have gotten this. Nobody knows about mountains—you have to give them lots of time.) "Glory isn't supposed to be smooth. Don't get too sentimental about this glory thing, huh?"

SHASTA is a mountain of mystery.
You can see it for a hundred miles.
But it gives you the feeling that you're never actually close to it.
Its peak is nearly always veiled in clouds.
It looks solitary and withdrawn.
Maybe nobody has ever talked to it.
Mountains, like people, can become lonely.
Somebody should talk to that mountain.

Me: "You look tall, powerful and majestic. So you rose to the occasion once. Hah, hah!" (I don't think humor goes over very well with mountains.) "Some mountains are bigger than others. Are you jealous of one another?"

Mountain: "I don't know why. We're all different. Are people jealous of one another?"

I had to say, "Yes, And we're all different, too."

The mountain reared back quite a bit.

Me: "It looks like you would be proud."

Mountain: "No, just definite. I'm being definite. I know what I'm for. I'm not going to run out of dreams."

Ouch! I had more respect for the old boy after that. But I couldn't help pushing a point! "So you're going to take it lying down. Your castles and bastions and brooding giants up there—prehistoric animals, forms, unimaginable heights—people will come out here, and they will walk all over you. They will make camps on your foot and your stomach. They will climb you and claim you. You will be their mountain.

Mountain: "They don't claim us. They just test themselves. That's good. We end up being friends."

I didn't realize that mountains had feelings, and I was kind of ashamed. I apologized.

Mountain: "No hard feelings. Say, (and I thought it was kind of wistful), do you know what kind of heaven there is for a mountain?"

Me: "No, I don't. It seems to me there was a promise somewhere."

Mountain: "It's a lot of waiting. You've got it better than we have. We'll wait. We've been here a long time."

I don't know why I asked this—maybe I felt something: "Are you ever afraid?"

Mountain: "Once we were afraid. Word got around—you know how word gets around—that people had come who could move mountains. Another human had told them they could. But there weren't any mountains moved. So we relaxed. This human, they say, walked on the water, too. If he did that, I guess he could teach people to move mountains. Do you know about this man?"

Me: "Sure I know him. I'm one of his personal friends."

Mountain: "Could you move a mountain?"

Me: (nervous) "Do you want to move?"

Mountain: "We have no orders to that effect."

Me: "I'll kind of think it over."

It is hard to realize how much there was to think about in what the mountain said.

The snow was drifted on the mountain in strange shapes. I was curious about that. Right there on the cliff, if you looked hard, you could see Don Quixote on his horse. Was that symbolic?

"What was that supposed to mean?" I asked the mountain.

Mountain: "Don Quixote."

There was another outline that looked like Snoopy lying flat on top of his doghouse.

Me: "Well, what does that represent?"

Mountain: "Snoopy."

It took a long time for the double "O" in Snoopy. I was beginning to feel foolish.

There was one configuration there—I said, "Oh, that could be either a monster or a bird, a beautiful bird. It could be the devil swooping down, or it could be an angel hovering."

Mountain: "Yes, it could be a devil or an angel."

At the moment, I felt frustrated and foolish, but I've thought a lot about that since.

So it went from one thing to another. It was uncomfortable, talking to a mountain. I didn't know whether I was standing on his eye or his head or his stomach. I asked him that.

Mountain: "Gee, you're kind of narrow-minded! What makes you think I've got a head? Mountains don't have to have a head just because you have one...I'm just round and big and everywhere."

Me: "You remind me of God. That's the way God is."

And the mountain said, "Thank you."

I tried to get that mountain to be my mountain, but he said he belonged to somebody already.

Now that I'm back at my desk, I don't know how this ever happened. If it ever happens to you, listen. Mountains talk slow, but they make good sense.

SECURITY: Go into your house.
Lock the doors and the windows.
Sit with a gun.
Listen for the sounds of Death
prowling outside.

TRUST: Give first.
Reach out before the other.
Put your love on the line.
Then life will come to you
not as a bargain but as a gift.

The Good Hang-Up

"Happy are the poor in spirit"...Scholars have given us many interpretations of this part of the Sermon on the Mount. Those who have studied the language in which Christ spoke his thoughts have now shed new light on the meaning of these words.

"Poor in spirit" does not mean poor in a money sense, and it does not mean poverty-stricken by itself. Neither does it refer to those who have plenty of money but are not too attached to their worldly goods. And, of course, "poor in spirit" does not mean worthless. No one of us is worthless in God's book. I want you to understand that. With us, *poor* sometimes has a belittling sound, as when we say "poor fool," "poor devil." To feel you are worthless—that's not even humility.

Nor does "poor in spirit" mean that we should be passive, mousey, without energy, without vision. "Poor in spirit" means that "it is in God that we live and move and have our being"...and we are happy about it. And isn't that the word— "*happy* are the..."

This kind of "poor" makes us dependent on God. We are privileged because dependent, dear to God because confident in him, and accepting dependence, unproud.

Are you getting the point? Our dependence is a willing and happy dependence. It makes us God's people. He is responsible for us. That is the only real meaning of "chosen race," "blessed people"—not blessed because we are great or proud, but because we are God's people by our own wanting it.

This brings us to a major problem of our life today, to a profound realization of a big modern mistake. The shock of modern technology has pushed us off balance. The achievements of science have step by step taken over our life. They tend to shrink the areas of mystery, of faith, and of that world beyond proof. Just compare honestly the difference between your confidence in prayer and in vaccine. You have proof of Salk's accomplishments; you have only a belief in God's caring for us. Science is apparently more dependable.

Analyze your feelings toward prayer and toward diet. Diet gets the pounds off; the scale proves that to you. Prayer gets results, too, but they don't compute very well.

So we pray less, or even stop praying. We let that reaching part of us pull back and we grab hold of the here and now. The touchable world is real because it *is* touchable, and the untouchable—by human hands—world fades.

But then what happens? We find ourselves in a mechanistic, transient, and therefore, in the long run, meaningless existence. The search for meaning ends in the blah distance of a burnt-out moon. The hunger for God is filled and killed with the cornhusks that unthinking animals live on.

Yet, like the Prodigal Son, we have memories of our Father's house where there are still things like goodness and honest anger and love around the table, and meaning beyond the stars at night.

The "poor in spirit" have not lost this memory and meaning. They are still real to the world they live in; they face its reality; they live life totally. They accept the gifts and challenges of man's need to live and to learn. They deal honestly with change and confusion and complexity. But they realize that God is still around, that he is creating in the work of human hands and revealing himself in every new frontier of human knowledge. They witness that God will not be pushed out of his own universe; that his love for us is underneath the atom and beyond the last conceivable star.

They say with the poet Rilke: "I believe in the sun even when it is not shining. I believe in love even when I am alone. I believe in God even when He is silent."

The Sermon on the Mount, where the Master blessed the poor in spirit, ends with Our Father. Do you know what you are asking for when you say the Our Father? Say it:

Our Father—in heaven—we bless your name and all that you are—may you take over our lives—may everything be done your way on earth just like it is done in heaven—give us today what each of us needs—and forgive us when we turn against you, as long as we forgive those who have turned against us—and don't let us be overcome by the power of evil—but be with us to the end.

This is not the way you are used to saying it, but this is what it means. Notice how much we depend on God for everything. If we mean that prayer deeply, we are "poor in spirit," leaning on God, his people, as trusting as a child swinging on his father's arm.

My Least Brother

Do you like to stand in line? I hate it. I've been trying to figure out why. I believe it's the real separation point between the "haves" and the "have-nots." It means you're not quite somebody. Anyway, I have a few things to say about standing in line.

I don't have to stand in line much, but the other day I had to go to the Social Security Office about some small matter—well, let's be honest—my application for Medicare. I gave my name to the lady at the desk, and she said, "Sit down over there." And I sat down over there, with the other people, and I waited.

An old fellow sitting across saw me—I was wearing my Roman collar (when you want to get a discount, or get service quicker, somehow you wear the collar)—this old guy came over—he could hardly talk because his lower jaw was so swollen. He smelled of you-know-what. He sat next to me and said, "I'm a Baptist, Father." I said "I'm a Catholic Father." I don't think either of us sounded as if we were ready to die for the Faith.

Anyway, he handled most of the conversation—it was nearly unintelligible—and told me how he went to the hospital and his stomach was full of gallstones and they operated on his jaw and did a bad job. To prove it, he grabbed my hand—a reluctant hand, to be sure—and put it under his chin so I could feel the tumorous growth there. He said, "You know, I have these squirrel pouches. I can't talk very good." I thought he might have done better with a little less of the bottle.

He slurred on about St. Joseph's Church and how he got help there. He also went to a church on 9th Street, where they gave out meal tickets. I nodded my head in that wise way you use when your mind is on something else. He was grateful even for that. I did ask him where he was from and whether he had a family, and he said, "No,—oh, yes, brothers and sisters." But he said it in a faraway voice. I could see they had brushed him off long ago. He told me how his dad got so despondent that he put two bullets "right there,"—he tapped over his right eyebrow. (I was wondering what the second bullet was for; the first would have been enough). He slurred on. One word kept coming out clear—"des-pon-den-cy"—long and slow, like a whole, sad lifetime. He looked at the floor.

Hello, little brother.
Why are you dressed like this—
in clothes too small
and sandals made from worn-out tires?
Your eyes are the eyes of the poor.
You will not let us rest . . .

44.

I was getting nervous—a whole half hour of waiting! He said that sometimes he waited all day in line. I said, "It must be tough." And he said, "It makes the time pass."

I finally got up, as if to leave. Then the lady behind the desk bustled over and said, "Father Noonan?" "Yes." "You're next." I felt the eyes of the waiting people on my back.

Standing in line—it's an insult to one's dignity. You know the feeling. Do you want frustration? Stand in line in a supermarket with your one quart of milk, behind a woman with two carts of groceries and a baby. You want insult? Stand in line for the fingerprinting to get a driver's license. You want shame? Stand in line to pay a traffic ticket. I was in one, and an irate citizen coming back from paying his fine looked at me and said, "The crooks! They're even taking money from the Church!" You want anxiety? Stand in line at the airport ticket window, to see if you'll make it before the plane takes off. You want fear? Wait in the dentist's office and listen to the stinging song of the drill.

This is the way I felt about it, too, until this morning. A funny thing happened to me while I was making my bed— one of the few things I have in common with people who stand in line. It struck me that we don't like it because it makes us feel second-rate, like servants. And that's just what we should be—servants.

Standing in line is our chance to share the situation of our brothers and sisters. It's an opportunity to let them feel our charity. I failed the old fellow in the Social Security Office. Maybe a few words of genuine interest would have made a real difference to him, given him some kind of lift. How many of us standing in the supermarket line would have told that mother what a pretty baby she had? Or tried to keep it from falling out of the cart? Or worked in some kind of a joke for the man next to us in the driver's license line? Or tried to soothe the ire of our neighbor in the traffic court? Or relieve the anxiety of the fellow behind us at the ticket window? Or, in the dentist's office, at least say a prayer for the patient under that drill?

St. Francis of Assisi found out what it was to be really poor by standing in a line of beggars outside a church in Rome. Christ went even farther than that. He *went* under the line, to wash the feet of a row of fishermen.

He challenged us to be a servant community. We can take that in the abstract and keep looking around for a great cause to serve—some day. Or we can look into the eyes of the brother or sister standing next to us in line.

Daddy, there's a tiger over there.   Where?

Right over there in the bushes.   That's a make-believe tiger.

Oh, make-believe tigers are the worst kind!   If it jumps out at us, what will we do?

Don't be scared. I won't let it hurt you.

And Jesus Went Home

One day, when Jesus was talking to the people, he spoke in parables. It was hard work, saying enough without saying too much. At the end of the day, Matthew says: "Leaving the crowds, he went home."

That never struck me before, but now I see it's a great, great statement. It's a tribute to the humanness, the man-quality in Jesus. "He went home." He had a home, you know. Sometimes we don't think of that. He had a home. I'm sure Matthew could have said more: "Jesus worked all day, walking the roads of Judea, or Galilee, and at night, he went home. Jesus was out curing the sick and the blind and the lame and the lepers, and he was under great strain, because this was hard work, curing people, and after it was over, he went home."

And while all this was going on, he was also teaching his disciples. They were hard students. They couldn't get anything very right. That was tiring, too. So he went home to rest. But the disciples came to him there and they said, "That was wonderful, but what did it mean? Those others didn't understand it—they're saying funny things. What did it mean? You can tell us."

And Jesus said to them, "Oh, what's the matter with you? Don't you know I have to speak in this deep, human way so that they will finally see it and believe? They've closed the front door, so I have to go around and come in the back door and I'm in the house before they know it."

He was home when he talked to them like this. These were his friends, and home was where his friends had access to him, where he gathered around him those who loved him and whom he loved. His mother must have been there. I think the house must have been regulated well; the food must have been lovingly fashioned. But the main thing is that it was home. He belonged there. In a special way, he belonged.

And I think he is telling us in this fashion that home should be a very meaningful thing to us. I mean the practical, real, physical home that we have. What is it like? Does it reflect our presence, my presence? Whatever member of the family we are, how does that home reflect our belonging? Is it a good place to be? A happy place, a peaceful place? Is it a place that is free of harsh words, loud talking, arguments? Those wouldn't be necessary as long as people could come together in love, fortify each other, understand each other's imperfections, each other's shortcomings, human defects, lacks.

What do you see in the eyes around you in the family circle? Do you see respect or fear? Do you see honesty or evasion? Do you see interest or boredom? This is something to study. After all, if you are a loving person, you will not be boring. You will be a little easy on the other members when it's necessary; when you see that there is hurt, a real hurt, and negligence, dereliction, abandonment.

Do you put restrictions on others? Do you create in them a need to be unhappy in their own lives? Do you arouse in them a tension, an uneasiness? Do you allow young people to grow up around you, spoiled because you are afraid of them, or because you are not interested in them, or you love them too much—that is, too possessively?

"And Jesus went home." You can imagine the expression on the faces of the people in that house when he opened the door. And how about your house, when you walk in?

Parent:
    "How many times have we told you
    not to bother us so early in the
    morning?!!"
Child:
    "I didn't come to bother you—
    I came to give you a kiss."

The Dance Of The Old Ones

Do you have a time of depression just before Christmas? Or is there something wrong with me? Maybe it's trying to be all things to all people that gives us that ragged feeling. We know how much it would mean to Aunt Mary to have a card or a present, and there's Uncle John, and cousins that we reckon up by dozens and—it's too much! So you get depressed.

What to do about it? Well, you say, "Hang in there!" But that has to be the worst advice there is.

Or you can do like I'm doing this late afternoon—come to Palisades Park in Santa Monica to look at the joggers. This is a strip of grass, like a green tape stretched along the edge of the cliffs above the beach. Palm trees and shrubs line the way. It's long—about two miles—it's narrow, and somehow it fills you with the urge to run from one end to the other. There must be twenty people of one shape or another doing it now.

Now, back to depression—wait, look at that runner just going by! He's sort of sliding, like a cat close to the ground, and he has a strange smooth motion, like in a ballet. I guess he just enjoys the feel of running. It reminds me of a dream I had, where I was running across the beach, I think. There was a cushiony feeling in my feet, not like the way I run now, where the feet go stumping along, without resilience and heavy in the heels.

Why do they pick on this long stretch instead of a square piece of land? Even I myself feel the urge to go the length. You know, there is something to being able to see the end of the race, not going around and around on a track. That turns me off. It's making a job out of an adventure.

I like to watch the faces of the joggers. When a person runs, somehow you see the meaning in his life, the wanted thing, a reaching out beyond what is...but now there is one who looks like he is on an assembly line, sort of compulsive, being driven— "just block it off and do it." There is some kind of reward, but no joy in it. He's afraid to stop and think, or the meaning of life might crush him. I feel sorry for him.

Oh, look, who is coming—the hurdler—the reaching out and the long stride, the floating, the joy of movement, the dance. It might be a good idea to pray that he takes the real hurdles of life like that.

The sun is going down now. The feeling of the moment and the place—the sky is striped with clouds, sort of swirled around like in an egg beater. The bright sun has simmered down into just a pot of gold, boiling over. It's a joyful sunset. It says, "Here comes tomorrow."

There are walkers, too, but they go barefoot. That's something. I suppose they want to feel the touch of the grass, the cold, spiky feeling between their toes. That lady—or late girl—getting a little wide—she's been back and forth two or three times now, barefooted. I guess she's throwing off the routine, the grubbiness of an office job, soaking up the green life of the grass.

I'm sorry—I ought to concentrate on our subject—depression...here's a man who's walking down the path, putting his feet down with great deliberation, like he is squashing bugs. He is old; he staggers a bit; he talks to himself and makes gestures with his hands. He must be telling some politician off.

It's too much to resist. It's a magic time. I walk along the palisade and I soak in the whole scene. The sun is turning more and more flarey, blooming out over the sea, and the colors are incredible. There are people standing near the edge, looking down at the steep dropaway, and I hear one of them say in a mournful accent: "Some day dis whole ting is going to go."

There's a couple just coming back from a stroll, and they're preposterous. An old man—he must be in his 80's—wearing a bright green beret, an orange windbreaker, dark pants and buckskin shoes. He towers over the ancient lady beside him. She is dressed all in red, with an Australian campaign hat, curled on the side. They toddle across the street, he in his brilliant ensemble, and she with her thin, woodeny legs, stumping along. And they're holding hands. Imagine that—after all this time, they're just proud to be together.

I look up at the tall, thin circle of palm trees. The moon is almost full in the cooling sky. The trees are a circus parade of clowns on stilts, making fingers against the sky—I wish I could recapture the feeling that comes to me about the sunset—the sky is blowing up with color, a dance of joy, dance of hope, the top clouds like windswept hair, gold and red.

A lady comes running across the grass, toward an old couple on the edge of the cliff. She calls, they move jerkily toward her, and the three faces light up in the sun. She says, "Isn't it wonderful to have all this?"

Next there is a young couple standing arm in arm, looking down onto the beach and the highway. I used to resent young couples in love, but not any more. And I sneak them a blessing.

Well, I was supposed to be writing about depression. But something happened to me out here, and all I can think of is that the richness of life is all around us, if we will only take time to park and look at it. It's not just in the sunset; it's in the shadows, the silhouettes, the crooked limbs, the young love and the dance of the old.

I'll tell you more about depression when I'm not feeling so good.

Keep a
green bo
in your
and the
singing b
will com
CHINESE PR

The Land Within

(Prayer is like scuba diving. You have to experience it—that fantastic undersea world, only faintly real to those who have never gone down and experienced the green and other-world depths. I put down these thoughts on prayer in an attempt to take you into that other world. It's our own only when we find it.

To understand the words I use, you have to go between the lines and the meaning, even between the words. In fact, you had better read these thoughts with your eyes closed, because I am saying something that cannot be said in words. Now, reading with your eyes closed is a little difficult, I admit. Perhaps you could use these musings in a group, and one could read for the rest. We search together, anyway.)

Prayer is the land within. Here is where we find God. But we must venture deep into that land and go far, go far from all that we have ever known. And we must do it alone. Our exploration of ourselves, our inner consciousness, calls for time and sacrifice. To make time for the journey, we may have to cut short the hours we spend on our distractions, even those we consider as necessary relaxation—sports, TV watching, talk time, side trips, dinners out. We may even have to take some time from our work, even our unselfish work, which can be our most soothing escape from the responsibiity of prayer (shouldn't this time be spent helping people?)

We drop off the excuses at the border and start into the land of our own self. It is a rough landscape, jagged with barren hills of pride, pitted with valleys where monsters live. We have felt them stirring within us, but this is the first time that we have dared to admit their presence, turn our eyes directly on them, no matter how the sight of them makes us cringe, half in fright and half in guilt at having become accustomed to them. And we must acknowledge that they have to be destroyed, however deep the pain because they have become part of us. The hills of pride must be leveled, the valleys filled in, and the way of the Lord made straight.

For help here are our own talents and gifts. For one of us, it is a bent toward nature—the sea and the mountains speak to us of God. For one with the mind of a mathematician, it is the ordered process of figures; for another, it is art or music. While we plunge farther into the subconscious, we condition our bodies and minds into quiet with helps like yoga or charismatic Christianity.

Our journey is from here to there
From where we are
To where we were meant to be.

There is always the temptation to pull back from the journey. We may have to struggle for what seems an eternity across arid stretches where there seems no hope of ever finding God. We become desperate for something to satisfy our hunger and thirst. On the horizon there appear oases that promise satisfaction and the slaking of all desire. These could be a fascination with nature, a diving into our work, love of another human being. But when we have grasped at the satisfaction, it vanishes. It was nothing but a mirage. We are left hungry, thirsty, and holding a handful of dust.

But then, often in the depths of a valley, we catch a glimpse of God. We know that it is He, and we know what we know. We rest on that conviction like tired travelers. The blaze of the vision has lighted up the landscape of our being. But then we see more faults and flaws, like thickets that we must remove. With each clearing, the path grows smoother, and the vision of God, the knowing, grows stronger.

Then one day we know that he is in us and around us; we move, breathe and live in his presence. Prayer, talking to God, is as natural as breathing. Then we can bring things from the world outside into this land, and find them not a distraction but a cause for prayer. Our work, the people we love and who love us, the small things that give us pleasure, the things that heighten our vision of God—admiration of the beauty he has put in the world, his gifts of mountain and sea especially, that speak to us of Him; art, music, good people. And we use also the things that help us understand better the sadness that is our vocation to lift from so many. We grow on books, films, music.

When we have talked to God, we fall silent. And at the core of our being, we listen to Him, we experience Him and his love. We let Him, however much it hurts, draw us farther from our old world into this new land with Him. Now to pray there is no crossing of a threshold, no knocking at a door between living and prayer. Prayer is our living with God. It is being at home in his presence.

Hello, In There!

I was at Old Mission Santa Barbara, in our time of theological renewal and meditation. One day I was walking around the garden, and I found myself near the vault where our Franciscan friars are buried. And it suddenly struck me that here in this vault are men whom I knew. I looked at the names.
Fr. Joseph, Fr. Thaddeus, Fr. Theophilus—just names now, and a residue of their humanity.

I began to think of my own life in terms of these men. They are beyond my touch now, except in prayer. But when they were with me, how did I use my gift of humanity with them? Fr. Joseph—we were good friends most of the time, but there were occasions when we had difficulty getting along. There was the time when, in a moment of give and take in the friar's dining room, I gave an imitation of Joe. I had been at lunch in the Biltmore coffee shop when he came striding in, Homburg on his arm, greeting all and sundry with an aristocratic air of the Spanish grandees whose descendant he was. I meant it for a joke, but he was hurt, deeply. And then there was Fr. Thaddeus, who was a great builder, and starved for someone to recognize his work. But I was too critical. And Brother Leopold, with whom I enjoyed life. I didn't give him enough understanding, though, enough appreciation, when he was risking his life running up and down the ladder at the high altar in St. Joseph's Church. And I remember one time saying something about his dogs—he loved dogs—being stupid. That hurt him more than anything else I could have said. But I was aloof from his hurt.

Here they all are—dead—and a name on a box is all that is left of them.

And I think of my life in terms of these brothers of mine. There has been much failing, much less love than I could have given. Then I think, well, they don't hold it against me now, as they take a calm, happy view of a world that's spinning. I put my hand on their name, and I ask their pardon for all lack, for all hurt.

I think of the open pockets in this vault. They are going to be filled with friars I know—perhaps soon. In the here and now, I can try harder to be a help to them and a lift toward a happy eternity. I think of the great potential I have to be Christ-like, if I can only live up to it.

Those open spaces—they're going to have names. I see mine on one of them. What's going to happen between now and the time my name goes up on the marker? How am I going to write my name there? Am I going to write in dead, cold letters, or am I going to write in happy memories left behind, in people I have shown love to, and places where I have helped?

Yes, it's a good meditation, and I pass it on to you, because each one has the same kind of challenge. Time is going to bundle us all into eternity, in one way or another, sooner or later.

The past we might be sorry for, but if we live Christ-like in the present, that past will be adorned and beautiful, and whatever future we have will be a singing in the night of the world, a singing toward the dawn.

At the Ninth Hour

Vacation was over. I was heading west from Tucson, across the trackless desert of southern Arizona.

I was traveling on a beautiful freeway which stretches across that part of the state, an endless straight road with very little traffic on it. There were absolutely no habitations, just miles and miles of flat country with occasional craggy peaks or ranges in the distance, and the organpipe cactus standing everywhere like stiff witnesses to the sun.

As I was going along, thinking to myself, letting the beauty and the space drift into my spirit, I saw far ahead a plume of smoke that stood straight up from the floor of the desert. It rose into the sky until it reached a certain level, and then it began to spread out. Somehow it was a new look at the mystery of creation. What struck me was the tremendous presence behind this item of nature—that this smoke, a completely inanimate thing, would have a law of its own and a place to be in the general scheme of creation; that smoke would rise to a certain height, and then, because of the laws that govern its being, it would thin out to a benign canopy over the earth.

It led me to think of the presence of God, his power; how he has set limits in his earth, and they are blessings. Man has limitations, too, but he has a tendency to go beyond them. He sends up so much smoke that it becomes like Cain's sacrifice—it comes down again in ashes and pollution. He puts too much smoke into the air, and darkness comes down at noon.

Man has to be content with his own limitations. He has to learn to be content if he cannot be completely satisfied in his desires. But man receives a beautiful gift from God and he wants more. His desires go beyond what he can have and he becomes spoiled in his own mind. He often feels that he has to blow out the boundaries, break the limitations with drugs or drink or anything else he thinks will expand him.

As I thought about these things, coming across the desert from Tucson, I remembered that I was coming back to begin another year of living and work. This is always a time for hope, the reaching up for better things. Another thought came—what is hope? Is it knowing that there won't be any cancer or hunger or loneliness this year? That wars will end? That the earth will cleanse itself of pollution? That there will be no unemployment—things like that?

No, hope means that the sun will come up; that the earth will show traces of spring; that men somewhere, some time, will act like brothers. Hope is not really in the earth or in the seasons, or in the ups and downs of gravity. It is in us. Even if the sun were not to rise, God is only a little harder to find in the dark. Even if the earth were to stop turning, the heart that hopes would spin on singing through space. 🍂 🍂 🍂

Hope means that you—and I—can stand like tall and stubborn cacti in our appointed ground, witnesses to the sun even when it burns.

To Francis of Assisi, all creatures were his brothers and sisters, because God was their father, to
Learning his wisdom, we can talk with water
          and space
          and people
             and clams
             and flowers
             and mountains and the rest.

               And all the lovely world will talk to us.

Of Time and the Music

My new clock radio fascinates me. It works by gravity. The little leaves have numbers on them, and they drop down. They are like the leaves of autumn, the leaves of life. Each minute makes a little "blipping" sound as it falls-"That's it, brother!"— BLIP! There's something about this clock. On most clocks, the hands go around, always moving. With this one, you see the time:—say it's 10:53. You stare at it, and nothing happens. Then you turn your head—BLIP!—it's 10:54. It's hard to catch the blipping. The blips count all the minutes of all the hours, to the end of time.

It's called a digital clock. "Digital" comes from the Latin, and it means finger. The clock is like a finger, pointing out something.

It points out the hours when you're asleep—blip, blip, all night long. It wakes you up, too, with the radio. How lovely to float into consciousness on the wings of music! But I had trouble with that. The first morning I tried using the music alarm, the station must have played Brahm's lullaby, because I never did wake up. I just had a musical dream. The second morning I woke up standing straight up in bed. Why would a station play "When the Saints Go Marching In" at six o'clock in the morning?

Anyway, things that go "blip" in the night say "Wake up!" in the morning. The blip is pointing out: if you don't know what to do with the morning hours, that's bad. Not to want the morning hours is not to want life. Sleep is a great temptation to people who are tired of trying, who have lost someone, or who don't want to face the things God has given them to do. So they sleep. People who are old have great temptations that way—why not just relax and die away? Sometimes all of us are tempted to escape into sleep, like the apostles in the garden when Christ was sweating blood. BLIP! BLIP! Wake up! Morning is for praying; bless the new day!

Even when I go out about my business, the clock keeps blipping. BLIP! Here's the busy executive on the freeway. I—don't we all—go too fast from where we were to where we will be. But that way we miss the turnoff to where we are. We have to double back through the baffling side streets, and when we get back, the present isn't there any more. We throw away the present. We can't be patient with time, and so we lose it. But time nips us in the end—BLIP! BLIP! We're not doing God's work that way; we're not fulfilling God's plan. And we don't have time to stop and listen to another's heart. Our necks stretch out longer and longer, straining. We don't go any faster; we just look like giraffes.

BLIP! Another point—maybe you're like me—I'm rushing off to an appointment. I'm late starting; I jump in the car. I don't have time to look at the address—oh, it's in Burbank. That's simple. But Burbank turns out to have a lot of streets. So I get lost. I stop in at a gas station and ask for Hickory Street. It must be around here somewhere. The service station man has just moved here from Iowa. He'd like to know where Hickory Street is, too. He looks it up on his map (why can't he move faster?) and then he says, "Oh, yes, go three signals down, and turn right, and then it will be—" I say, "Oh, yes, Oh, yes, I've got it now!" And you know how it goes—by the time I get to the next signal, I realize I never did listen to what he was saying. So I'm lost again. BLIP—the finger is pointing. Join the club. We don't realize our limitations. We try to do the things we can't do and we won't let others help us, not even God. "That's a mistake," says the blip. "Admit your weaknesses; pray for the wisdom to know what you can't do, and for the strength to do what you can."

Oh, I've got a clock-full of blips to share with you! But here's the last one for now. The blips count all the minutes of all the hours. Morning, noon and night. But, sooner or later, the last minute will fall—BLIP! And that's all right, so long as our clock is set for music.

🐞 🐞 🐞

Thoughts At Sunset

I was giving a Sisters' retreat at Marymount in Santa Barbara. Marymount is a house of prayer, on the farther side of the long hill that rises above the city.

The Sisters came in small groups, their faces wearing the shadow of work, probing each other's smiles for the feel of home—the not quite captured familiness, but always wanted; reaching for each other out of the haze of separation, and beginning to fit feelings with sighs together.

Haze drifted along the high hills like the tint on a windshield (no, I carried that metaphor from the nervous freeway). What I want to say is that the far hills were smokey blue, the ridges in faint outline, but lower down the sun was a golden surf washing on green—healing the hurt hills, washing them young again.

The sun was low and soft on the trees around the house. When leaves are against the sun like that, all lit up and trembling with color, it makes me think of God, a burning presence in common things—setting simple things on fire with an inner life.

Those bougainvillea clusters in the patio—impossible—yes, the vine could grow; yes, it could bloom, but to suck that incredible color out of the dark ground—never! It just bleeds into the air, with a life not its own. Something strange is going on there. It happens—well, it happens. For me mysticism is easier than mathematics.

This place is out-of-words beautiful. Green-green; green on green. A loping lawn. Brown quail sneaking out of the ivy under the green trees. Quail are such busy creatures and so scared...they are the people we know who strut and run. They are busy to be shy, and they need our patient waiting to come out of the trees again. They need us to be the warm, brown birds that have the smoothest, swiftest flight.

Somehow Job's wonder gets into me. I wonder why he was not happier.

Who put the shininess in the magnolia leaves
or curved them so?
Who put the rainbow in the sprinkler,
or gave the rhythm to its rain?
Who taught the butterfly to write in the air
and to tell us beauty is not a straight line?

By the upper road, there are other trees above the green ones. Some are eucalyptus waving arms against the sky; some are oaks arching darkly along the hill, hooded prophets saying "There is more."

In the convent infirmary, a great lady is dying. Old. Quiet. Her sisters stand around loving her, letting her go, (Death makes sense out of life—yours and mine)...the sun making shadows and silhouettes of tenderness...the dying sun dancing at the window.

Cast your net into each new day
and gather in the teeming catch
of opportunities and dreams.